NEXT STATION 2

STUDENT'S BOOK

Amanda Cant / Mary Charrington
Sarah Elizabeth Sprague

macmillan education

CONTENTS

CHARACTERS AND ICONS

LOOK AND DO / LISTEN AND DO

Activities to interpret the picture of the unit opener pages

LISTEN

Audio tracks to practice listening skills

WORLD MUSIC

Songs with a World Music flavor

TEMPLATE

Photocopiable Language File activities to use in class

BE sociable and creative.
Know yourself!

THINK critically when you use information!

LEARN to do things by yourself.
Learn how to learn!

COLLABORATE / COMMUNICATE with others. Teamwork is cool!

ACT respectfully, be tolerant, and friendly!

·WELCOME TO NEXT STATION!·

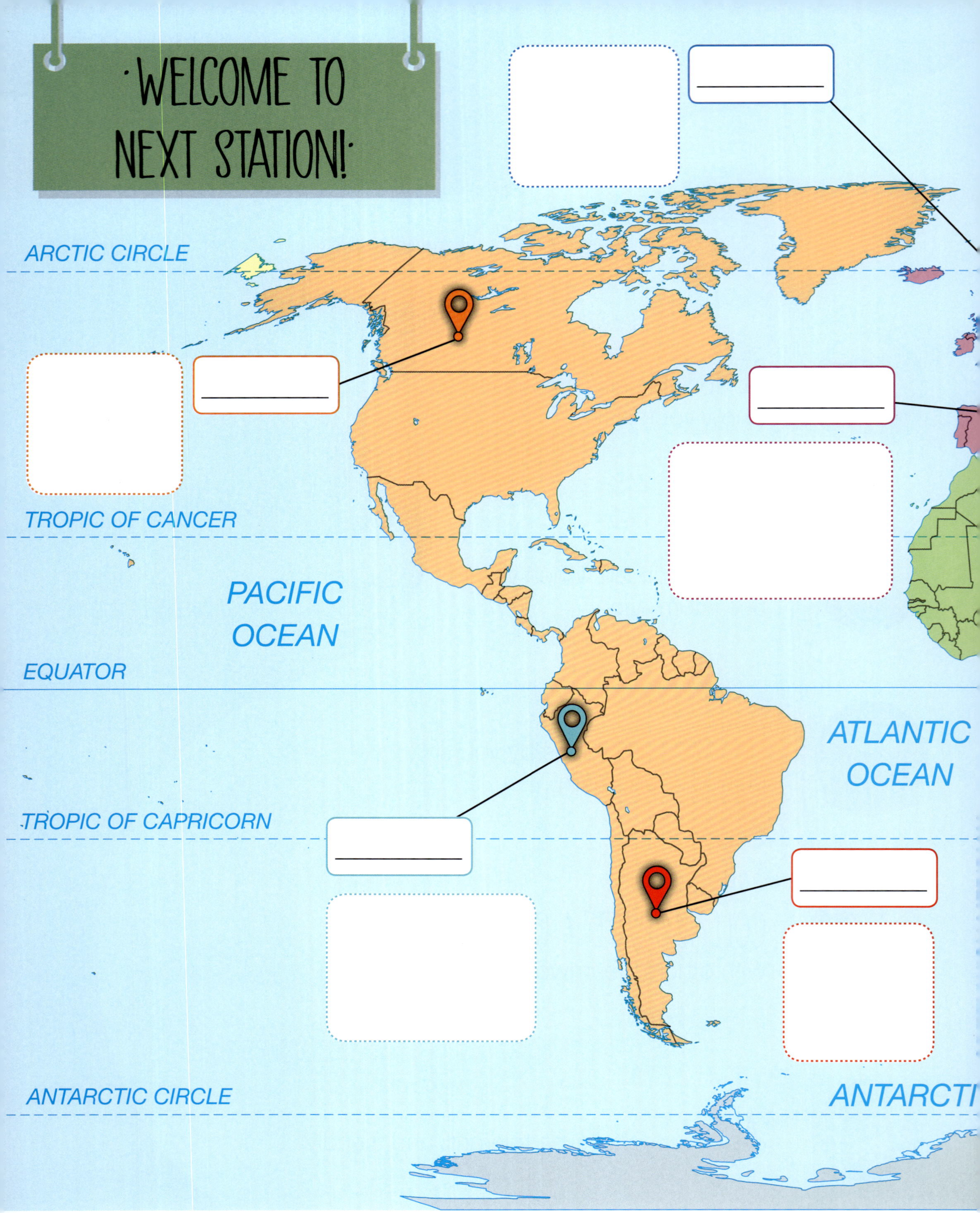

Africa

America

Antarctica

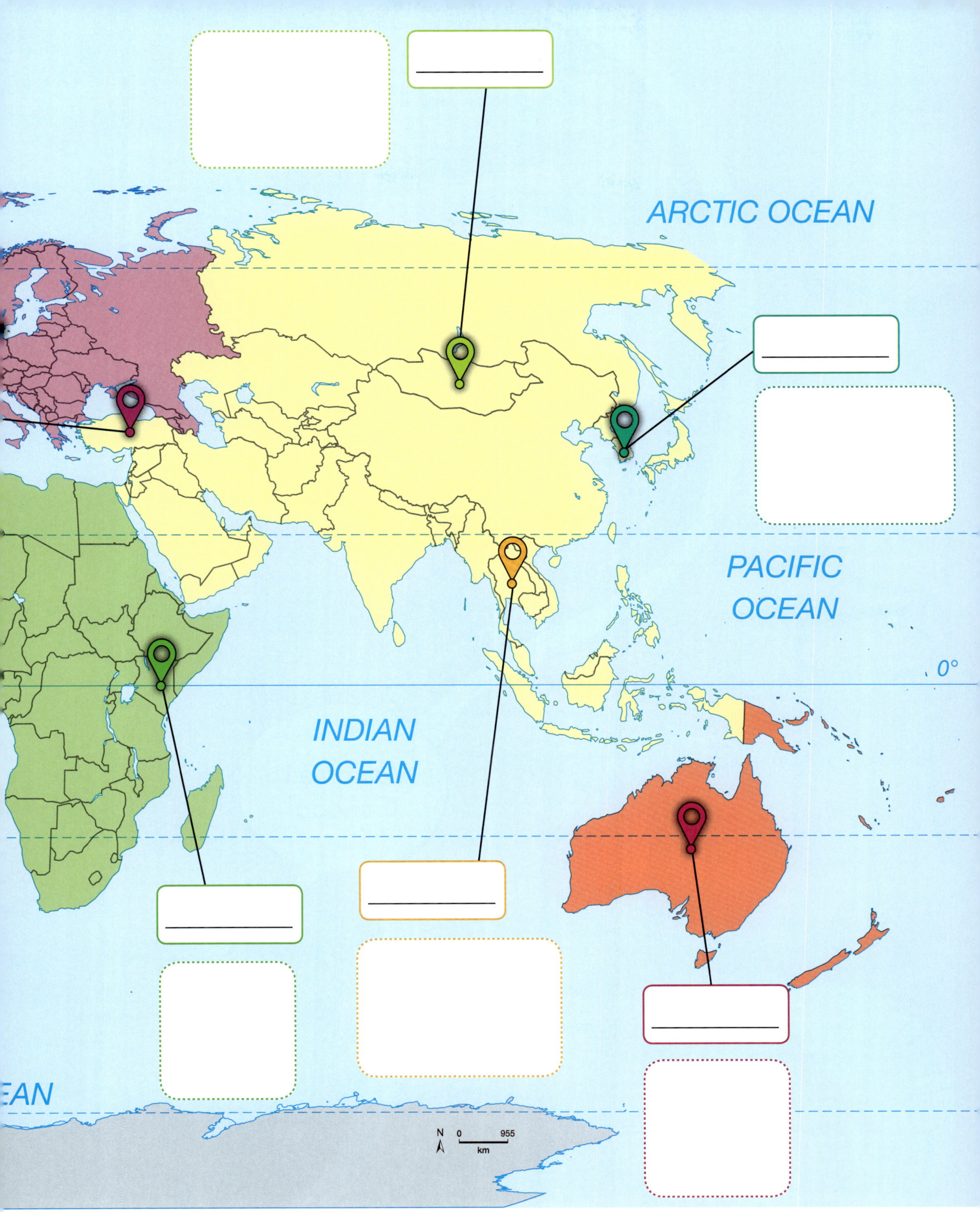

Asia

Europe

Oceania

CANADA

UNIT 1

Look at the picture and circle.

There are **pandas** / **brown bears** in the **mountains** / **towns** in Canada.

UNIT 1

Lesson 1

VOCABULARY

TRACK 2

1 Listen, point, and say.

3 talk

5 shout

2 sit down

4 clean up

1 stand up

6 run

2 Look and circle.

1 shout / clean up

2 talk / run

3 stand up / sit down

3 Play the Action Game.

WORKBOOK
page 4

GRAMMAR

Don't shout.
Sit down, please.

TRACK 3

1 Listen, read, and say.

2 Number in order.

1 up, ◯ please. ◯ Clean ◯

2 down. ◯ Don't ◯ sit ◯

3 Play the Please Game.

WORKBOOK page 5
GRAMMAR GUIDE page 129

· SOUNDS GREAT ·

TRACK 4

1 Listen and chant.

Look at my cake!
It's a snake in a lake.
Take a plate!

TRACK 5

2 Listen and say.

ake **ate**

cake

plate

snake

lake

3 Look and write.

_____ _____ ake

_____ _____ ate

_____ ake

_____ ake

4 Read the chant and underline *ake* and *ate*.

WORKBOOK page 6

·READING TIME·

TRACK 6

1 Listen and read.

2 Read the story again. Check (✓) the value.

Eat fruit. ◯ Be polite. ◯

3 Circle the polite words. Do you use these words?

please / don't / thank you / sorry / cherries

WORKBOOK page 7

VOCABULARY

TRACK 7

1 Listen, point, and sing. **The ABC Song**

1 A B C D E F G

2 H I J K L M N

3 O P Q R S T U V

4 W X Y Z

2 Ask and answer.

Yellow, 3.

Brown, 4.

S.

Y.

TEMPLATE 1

3 Complete. Then write the secret words.

WORKBOOK page 8

Lesson 6

GRAMMAR

How do you spell "snake"?

TRACK 8

1 Listen, read, and say.

2 Number in order.

do ◯ spell ◯ you ◯ How ◯ "dog"? ◯

3 Ask and answer.

How do you spell "clock"?

C-l-o-c-k.

WORKBOOK page 9
GRAMMAR GUIDE page 129

LET'S VISIT CANADA

1 Read about national favorites from Canada.

Hi, I'm Sara.
My favorite sport is ice hockey. It's the national sport of Canada. Let's play, OK? Don't sit down! It's cold. Skate with me, please. It's fun!

This is a beaver. It's the national animal of Canada! Beavers are brown and have black eyes. They're cute! There are lots of beavers in Canada. Are there beavers in your country?

Think Twice

1 Circle.

Ice hockey / **Soccer** is the national sport of Canada.

The **brown bear** / **beaver** is the national animal of Canada.

2 What is the national sport of your country?

SPEAKING TIME

1 Draw, write, and say.

The national animal of Canada is a beaver. What's the national animal of your country?

NEW FRIENDS

1 Complete the conversation. Choose your response.

Hi! I'm Sara. What's your name?

My name's ______________________.

How do you spell your name?

______________________.

2 Act out the conversation.

WORKBOOK page 10

UNIT 2

GERMANY

TRACK 9

Listen and find the clock.

UNIT 2

Lesson 1

· VOCABULARY ·

TRACK 10

1 Listen, point, and say.

1 second

2 minute

3 hour

4 morning

5 afternoon

6 evening

TRACK 11

2 Listen and circle.

1 15 minutes / 15 seconds

2 7 minutes / 7 hours

3 5 seconds / 5 hours

3 Look, write, and act.

1 Good ____________________.

2 Good ____________________.

3 Good ____________________.

WORKBOOK page 11

Lesson 2

GRAMMAR

What time is it?
It's eight **o'clock**.

TRACK 12

1 Listen, read, and say.

TRACK 13

2 Listen, draw, and write.

1 What time ____________________?

It's ____________________.

2 What ____________________ is it?

____________________.

TEMPLATE 2

3 Make a clock. Ask and answer.

WORKBOOK page 12

GRAMMAR GUIDE page 129

UNIT 2

Lesson 3

SOUNDS GREAT

TRACK 14

1 Listen and chant.

Nine dimes in a line.
Look! One more dime.
One more time!

TRACK 15

2 Listen and say.

ime **ine**

time

dime

nine

line

3 Look and write the letters in order.

neil ____________

tmie ____________

ienn ____________

eidm ____________

4 Read the chant and underline *ime* and *ine*.

WORKBOOK page 13

READING TIME

TRACK 16

1 Listen and read.

2 Read the story again. Check (✓) the value.

Look at the time. ◯ Don't be late. ◯

3 How do you feel when you are late? Circle.

WORKBOOK page 14

UNIT 2

Lesson 5

VOCABULARY

TRACK 17

1 Listen, point, and say.

1 get up

2 have breakfast

3 go to school

4 have lunch

5 have dinner

6 go to sleep

TRACK 18

2 Listen and say what's next.

TRACK 19

3 Sing and act. **My Busy Day**

I get up and I have breakfast,
At the start of every day.
I go to school and I have lunch,
I work and then I play.
I have dinner with my family.
Then I have time to play.
I go to bed and I go to sleep.
It's a busy, busy, day!

WORKBOOK page 15

GRAMMAR

I get up at seven o'clock.

TRACK 20

1 Listen, read, and say.

2 Complete about you.

1 I have breakfast at ______________ o'clock.

2 ______________ go to school at ______________.

3 ______________ have dinner at ______________.

3 Play the Mime Game.

WORKBOOK page 16
GRAMMAR GUIDE page 129

LET'S VISIT GERMANY

1 Read about traditional food from Germany.

Hello! I'm Gunther. I'm from Hanover, in Germany.

Look at this! It's a traditional German chocolate cake! It's called Black Forest cake. It has chocolate, cream, and cherries. It's delicious. I eat chocolate cake in the afternoon and evening! Is it time for cake?

Think Twice

1 Read and check (✓).

Black Forest cake has chocolate, ◯ cream, ◯ trees, ◯ cherries, ◯ pears. ◯

2 When do you eat cake?

SPEAKING TIME

1 Draw, write, and say.

Mmm! Traditional chocolate cake from Germany ...

____________________ is a traditional dessert from my country.

NEW FRIENDS

1 Complete the conversation. Choose your response.

Would you like to try some Black Forest cake?

Yes, please. ◯

No, thanks. ◯

2 Act out the conversation.

WORKBOOK page 17

PROGRESS CHECK

1 Read, look, and write the numbers.

1 Clean up, please. **2** Sit down, please. **3** Don't talk. **4** Don't run.

2 Look, say, and write.

1  ______________________

3  ______________________

2  ______________________

4  ______________________

THINK AGAIN!

An animal from Canada is the ______________________.

My favorite lesson is on page ______________________.

The national sport of Canada is ______________________.

WORKBOOK page 18 STICKERS PASSPORT page 2

UNIT 2

PROGRESS CHECK

1 Read and draw.

1 It's three o'clock.

2 It's eight o'clock.

2 Look and write.

1 It's ______________________.

2 It's ______________________.

3 Look and complete.

1 I ______________________ at eight o'clock.

2 I ______________________ at twelve o'clock.

3 I ______________________ at seven o'clock.

4 I ______________________ at eight o'clock.

THINK AGAIN!

A famous food in Germany is ______________________.

My favorite picture is on page ______________________.

A traditional object from Germany is ______________________.

WORKBOOK page 19

STICKERS

PASSPORT page 4

CANADA

The Peace Tower clock in Ottawa, Canada.

Mythical figures adorn the building.

Gargoyles are decorative and help keep rain water away.

STEAM

TEAM NAME

Why do we need to know the time?

1 Get materials.

play dough

toothpicks

ruler

colored pencils

scissors

glue stick

paper

A clock tower has one or more clock faces.

The Peace Tower clock was a gift from the UK in 1927.

The clock of the New Town Hall was first heard in 1908.

CHALLENGE 1

BUILD A CLOCK TOWER

2 Look at the geometric shapes below. Draw your plan.

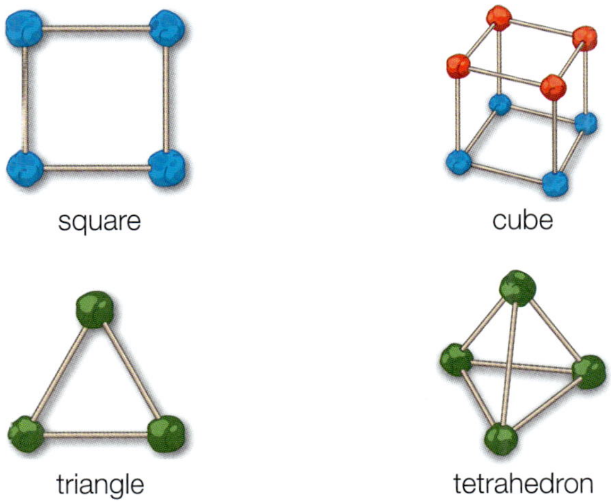

3 Build a clock tower.

4 Name your clock tower.

____

5 How tall is it?

_______________ cm

Did your clock tower match your drawing? Why or why not?

GERMANY

The clock tower of the New Town Hall in Munich, Germany.

The Glockenspiel, a tourist attraction at the New Town Hall.

Some of the 32 figures on the Glockenspiel stage.

TEAMWORK ★★★★★

KENYA

UNIT 3

24 NOV
KENYA
NAIROBI
INTERNATIONAL
AIRPORT

Welcome to Kenya!

Circle the three animals from Kenya.

TRACK 21

1 Listen, point, and say.

TRACK 22

2 Listen and guess.

3 Look and complete.

1 It's a ______________________.

2 It's a ______________________.

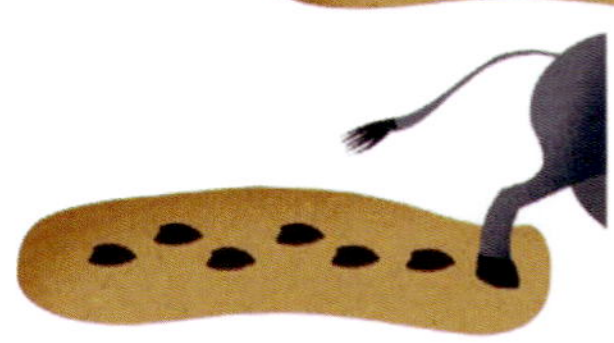

3 It's a ______________________.

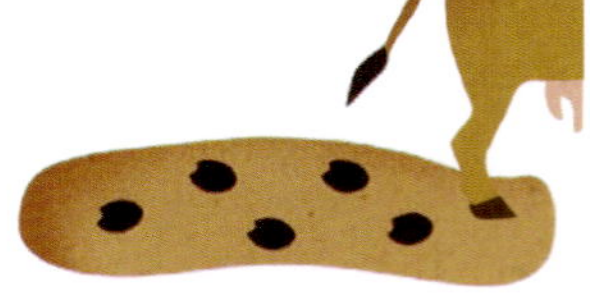

4 It's a ______________________.

WORKBOOK page 20

Lesson 2

GRAMMAR

This is a duck.
That's a cow.
These are goats.
Those are chickens.

TRACK 23

1 Listen, read, and say.

2 Look and circle.

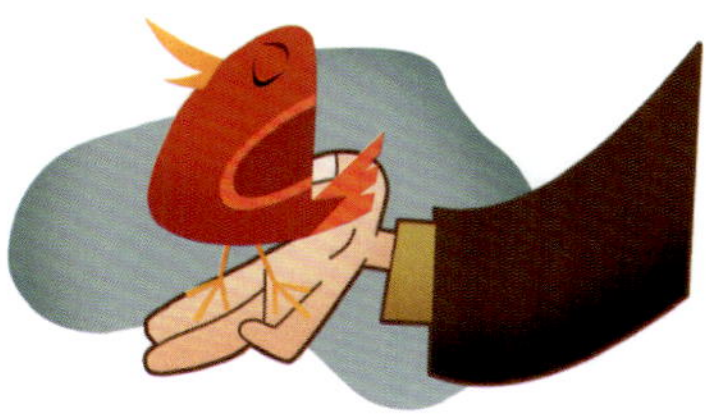

1 **This is** / **That's** a bird.

2 **These** / **Those** are chickens.

TEMPLATE 3

3 Draw and talk about your animals.

WORKBOOK page 21

GRAMMAR GUIDE page 130

UNIT 3

Lesson 3

SOUNDS GREAT

TRACK 24

1 Listen and chant.

The bone is under a stone
but his nose is in a rose!

TRACK 25

2 Listen and say.

one **ose**

bone

stone

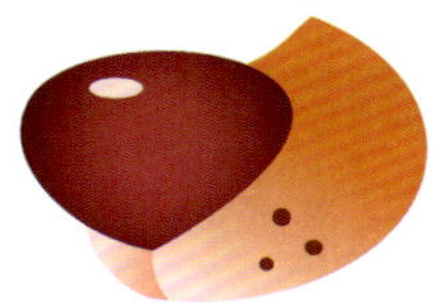

nose

rose

3 Connect and write.

1 s t o n e ____________________

2 n o s e ____________________

3 r o s e ____________________

4 b o n e ____________________

4 Read the chant and underline *one* and *ose*.

WORKBOOK page 22

·READING TIME·

TRACK 26

1 Listen and read.

2 Read the story again. Check (✓) the value.

Be responsible. ◯ Listen to your grandma. ◯

3 What responsible things do you do? Circle.

WORKBOOK page 23

UNIT 3

Lesson 5

VOCABULARY

TRACK 27

1 Listen, point, and say.

1 ladybug

2 grasshopper

3 caterpillar

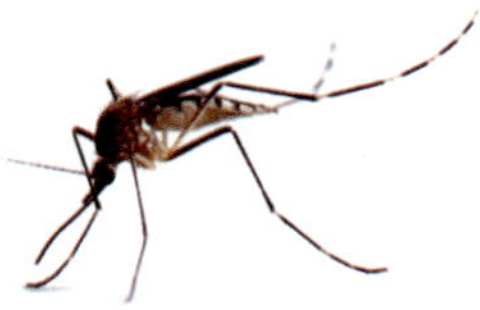

4 mosquito

5 butterfly

6 ant

2 Look and write.

1 These are ______________________.

2 This is a ______________________.

3 ______________________.

4 ______________________.

WORKBOOK page 24

GRAMMAR

What's this / that?
It's a caterpillar / **an** ant.
What are these / those?
They're grasshoppers.

TRACK 28

1 Listen, read, and say.

TRACK 29

2 Sing. **Itchy, Ouchy Mosquito**

What are these? What are these?
They're green grasshoppers.
What are those? What are those?
They're curly caterpillars.

What's that? What's that?
It's a shiny black cat.
And what's this? Ooh! Ouch! Stop! Oh, no!
It's an itchy, ouchy, itchy, ouchy mosquito!

WORKBOOK page 25

GRAMMAR GUIDE page 130

24 NOV KENYA NAIROBI INTERNATIONAL AIRPORT

LET'S VISIT KENYA

1 Read about animals in Kenya.

Hi! My name's Zalika. I'm from Kenya.

Kenya is famous for its animals. There are many different animals there. These are zebras. They're black and white. They are very similar to donkeys and horses.

Look at those giraffes! Wow! Their necks are long! Giraffes eat green leaves from trees for breakfast, lunch, and dinner! They love leaves.

What are these? They're birds! Pink birds! And they are called pink flamingos. They are very, very beautiful!

Think Twice

1 Read and write *z* (zebra), *g* (giraffe), or *f* (flamingo).

It's a bird. ◯ It's black and white. ◯

It has a long neck. ◯

2 Are there pink flamingos in your country?

SPEAKING TIME

1 Draw, write, and say.

This is a giraffe from Kenya.

This is a / an ____________________ from my country.

NEW FRIENDS

1 Complete the conversation.

I like giraffes, too. ◯

I prefer ____________________. ◯

2 Act out the conversation.

WORKBOOK page 26

UNIT 4

TURKEY

Check (✓) three things from Turkey.

1 ◯ 2 ◯ 3 ◯ 4 ◯

UNIT 4

Lesson 1

VOCABULARY

TRACK 30

1 Listen, point, and say.

1 peppers

2 potatoes

3 onions

4 carrots

5 beans

6 tomatoes

2 Count and write.

1 There are three peppers.

2 ______________________.

3 ______________________.

4 ______________________.

5 ______________________.

6 ______________________.

3 Ask and answer.

How many peppers are there?

There are three.

WORKBOOK page 27

Lesson 2

· GRAMMAR ·

Do you like carrots?
Yes, **I do**. / No, **I don't**.

TRACK 31

1 Listen, read, and say.

2 Complete and color your answer.

		Yes, I do.	No, I don't.
1	Do you like onions?	◯	◯
2	______ peppers?	◯	◯
3	______ beans?	◯	◯
4	______ potatoes?	◯	◯
5	______ tomatoes?	◯	◯

3 Ask and answer.

Do you like carrots?

No, I don't.

WORKBOOK page 28
GRAMMAR GUIDE page 130

UNIT 4

Lesson 3

· SOUNDS GREAT ·

TRACK 32

1 Listen and chant.

The boy plays a tune,
Under the moon.
And the girl eats prunes
With her spoon.

TRACK 33

2 Listen, say, and color.

une **oon**

spoon

prune

moon

tune

3 Write and match.

oon une

sp ___ ___ ___

t ___ ___ ___

m ___ ___ ___

pr ___ ___ ___

4 Read the chant and underline *une* and *oon.*

WORKBOOK page 29

·READING TIME·

TRACK 34

1 Listen and read.

2 Read the story again. Check (✓) the **value**.

Say "Thank you." ○ Try new things. ○

3 Look at the story and answer.

Do you try new things when you eat outside your house?

Do you like to try things that look unusual?

WORKBOOK page 30

UNIT 4

Lesson 5

VOCABULARY

TRACK 35

1 Listen, point, and say.

2 Match.

ice pops
French fries
sandwiches
pancakes
hamburgers
cookies

TEMPLATE 4

3 Write. Then ask and answer.

WORKBOOK page 31

GRAMMAR

I like hamburgers.
I don't like peppers.

TRACK 36

1 Listen, read, and say.

2 Talk to a friend.

beans	**carrots**	**cookies**
French fries	**hamburgers**	**ice pops**
onions	**pancakes**	**peppers**

I like ice pops.
I don't like onions.

TRACK 37

3 Sing. **I Like Food!**

Do you like hamburgers?
Yes, I do. Yes, I do.
I like hamburgers with onions.

Do you like bananas?
Yes, I do. Yes, I do.
I like bananas with hot pancakes.

Do you like everything?
No, I don't. No, I don't.
I don't like spiders and I don't like snakes!

WORKBOOK page 32
GRAMMAR GUIDE page 130

LET'S VISIT TURKEY

TURKEY
Türkiye Cumhuriyeti
Republic of Turkey

1 Read about food markets in Turkey.

Hello, I'm Ahmet, and this is my dad.

Look at his vegetable stand. There are peppers, beans, and tomatoes.

This is a traditional market in Turkey. There are many different foods here. And they are all fresh and delicious. Don't forget, eat lots of fresh vegetables!

This is a famous candy from Turkey. It's called Turkish delight. It's very sweet! And look at all the colors! Turkish delight is yellow, orange, or green!

Think Twice

1 What can you buy at the market? Circle.

cookies / beans / French fries / peppers / ice pops / tomatoes

2 Is there a similar type of food market in your town?

SPEAKING TIME

1 Draw, write, and say.

Turkish delight is a famous candy from Turkey. What candy is famous in your country?

____________________ is a famous candy from my country.

NEW FRIENDS

1 Complete the conversation. Choose your response.

Do you like candy?

____________________.

I have Turkish delight. Here, try one.

Thank you! ◯

No, thanks. ◯

2 Act out the conversation.

WORKBOOK page 33

UNIT 3

· PROGRESS CHECK ·

1 Look, read, and number.

That's a monkey.	1	Those are elephants.		This is a ladybug.	
These are snakes.		That's a butterfly.		These are caterpillars.	

2 Look and write.

~~What's this?~~ What's that? What are these? What are those?

1 What's this? ______ It's a ladybug.

2 ______ They're caterpillars.

3 ______ They're elephants.

4 ______ It's a monkey.

THINK AGAIN!

Two animals from Kenya are ______ and ______.

My favorite lesson is on page ______.

Giraffes love to eat ______.

WORKBOOK page 34
STICKERS
PASSPORT page 6

UNIT 4

PROGRESS CHECK

1 Complete and answer *Yes, I do.* or *No, I don't*.

1 Do you like  ____________? ____________.

2 Do you like 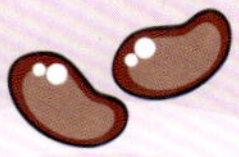 ____________? ____________.

3 Do you like  ____________? ____________.

4 Do you like 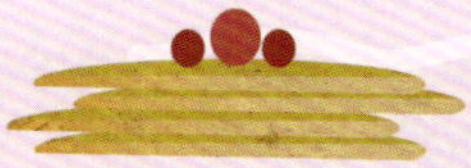 ____________? ____________.

5 Do you like  ____________? ____________.

2 Look and write.

	Niki	Bubba
1	I like tomatoes.	I don't like onions.
2	____________	____________
3	____________	____________

THINK AGAIN!

Two types of food from Turkey are ____________ and ____________.

My favorite picture is on page ____________.

A traditional object from Turkey is ____________.

KENYA

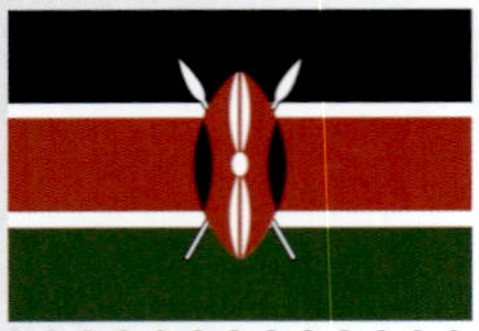

The arid region below Mount Kenya.

Samburo child in traditional clothing.

Camel in the Chalbi desert, Kenya.

STEAM

TEAM NAME

How many minutes does it take a camel to drink 113 liters of water? 13, 23, or 30?

1 Get materials.

paper squares

measuring cup with water

Dromedary camels have only one hump. The hump is full of fat.

Bactrian camels have two humps.

Camels can go 6 months without food or water. Their habitat is hot, dry, and sandy.

CHALLENGE 2

DESIGN A PAPER CUP

2 Design a paper cup. Follow the model.

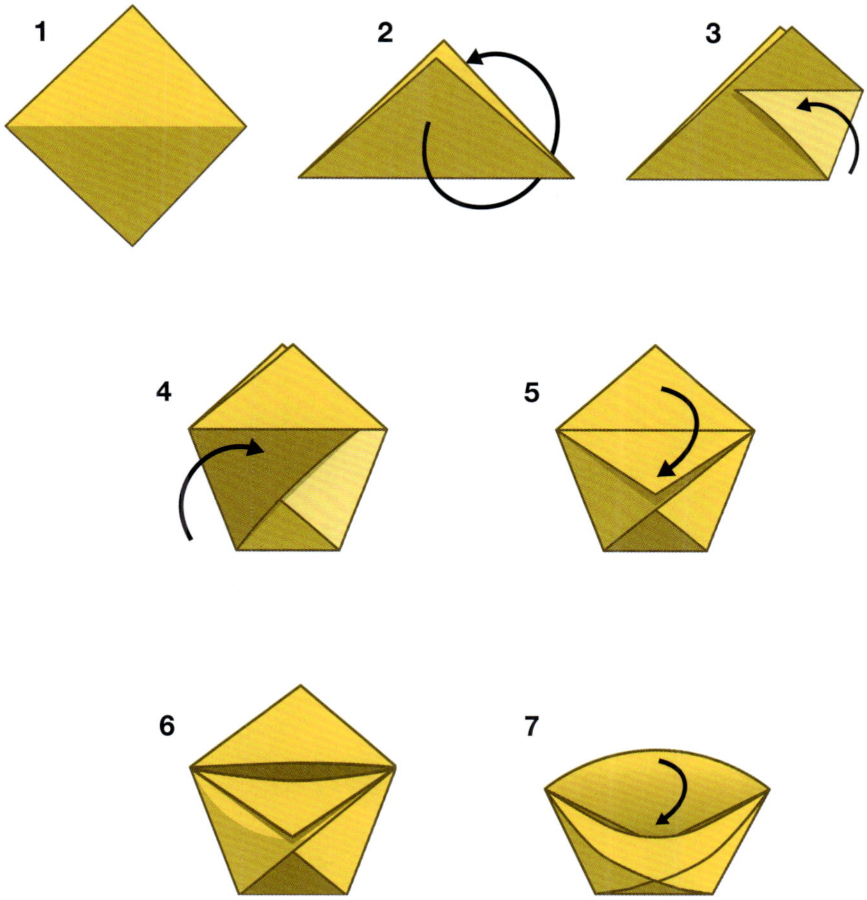

3 Fill it with water. Test your cup for 10 seconds.

How do you conserve water?

TURKEY

The semi-arid region of Cappadocia, in Turkey.

Turkish dancer in traditional clothing.

Camel with a child in Antalya, Turkey.

UNIT 5

SOUTH KOREA

TRACK 38

Listen and circle the music from South Korea.

1 2 3

Unit 5

Lesson 1

VOCABULARY

TRACK 39

1 Listen, point, and say.

2 Match and say.

do	rope
play	your toes
speak	the guitar
climb	a tree
touch	Vietnamese
jump	taekwondo

3 Play the Whisper Game.

WORKBOOK page 36

Lesson 2

GRAMMAR

Can you play the guitar?
Yes, **I can**. / No, **I can't**.

TRACK 40

1 Listen, read, and say.

2 Write.

1 Can you speak English? ______________________.
2 Can you climb a tree? ______________________.
3 Can you do taekwondo? ______________________.
4 Can you play the guitar? ______________________.
5 Can you jump rope? ______________________.

3 Ask and answer.

Can you speak Vietnamese?

No, I can't.

WORKBOOK page 37
GRAMMAR GUIDE page 131

Unit 5

Lesson 3

SOUNDS GREAT

TRACK 41

1 Listen and chant.

The teacher is under
A big, green tree.
"This is a bean.
Repeat after me!"

TRACK 42

2 Listen, say, and color.

ea **ee**

green

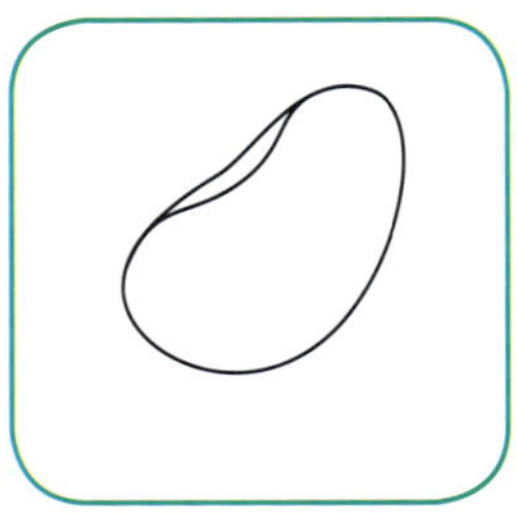

bean

teacher

tree

3 Write and match.

ea **ee**

t ____ ____ cher

gr ____ ____ n

b ____ ____ n

tr ____ ____

4 Read the chant and underline *ea* and *ee*.

WORKBOOK page 38

READING TIME

TRACK 43

1 Listen and read.

2 Read the story again. Check (✓) the **value**.

Play music. ◯ Be positive. ◯

3 What do you say when you are being positive?

No, I can't. ◯ Yes, I can. ◯

WORKBOOK page 39

Unit 5 Lesson 5

· VOCABULARY ·

TRACK 44

1 Listen, point, and say.

1 fly

2 swim

3 hop

4 sing

5 walk

6 ride a horse

2 Read and circle.

1 Can you swim?	Yes, I can. / No, I can't.
2 Can you hop?	Yes, I can. / No, I can't.
3 Can you walk?	Yes, I can. / No, I can't.
4 Can you fly?	Yes, I can. / No, I can't.
5 Can you ride a horse?	Yes, I can. / No, I can't.
6 Can you sing?	Yes, I can. / No, I can't.

TEMPLATE 5

3 Complete the quiz. Ask and answer.

WORKBOOK
page 40

GRAMMAR

I / He / She / They can sing.
I / He / She / They can't swim.

TRACK 45

1 Listen, read, and say.

TRACK 46

2 Sing and act. **I Can Do It!**

I can speak Vietnamese,
I can do taekwondo.
I can swim, I can hop,
I can touch my big toe.

I can play the guitar,
I can jump up high.
But I can't, no, I can't,
I just can't fly!

WORKBOOK page 41
GRAMMAR GUIDE page 131

LET'S VISIT SOUTH KOREA

1 Read about special events in South Korea.

Hi, I'm Jin. I'm from South Korea.

There are lots of festivals in South Korea. At the Moon Festival, some people play traditional games and eat special foods! People eat rice with nuts and beans. Do you like beans?

Dano is a Korean holiday. People sing traditional songs. They play drums and trumpets. They dance and play traditional games. And they wrestle! Can you wrestle?

Think Twice

1 Read and circle.

People eat special food at the Moon Festival. True / False

People play guitars on the Dano holiday. True / False

2 Can you name a special event in your country?

SPEAKING TIME

1 Draw, write, and say.

At festivals in my country, people eat / play

______________________________.

NEW FRIENDS

1 Complete the conversation. Choose your response.

I can do taekwondo. Can you?

- Yes, I can. ◯
- No, I can't, but I can ______________________. ◯

This is my sister. She can ride a horse. Can you?

- Yes, I can. ◯
- No, I can't. ◯

2 Act out the conversation.

WORKBOOK page 42

UNIT 6

ARGENTINA

Check (✓) three activities from Argentina.

1 

2 

3 

4 

UNIT 6 Lesson 1

VOCABULARY

TRACK 47

1 Listen, point, and say.

1 play soccer

2 watch TV

3 sing karaoke

4 play computer games

5 read books

6 play board games

TRACK 48

2 Listen and guess.

3 Check (✓) the activities in the pictures.

1 sing karaoke ◯
2 play soccer ◯
3 watch TV ◯
4 play board games ◯
5 read books ◯
6 play computer games ◯

WORKBOOK page 43

GRAMMAR

What do you like doing?

I like reading.

I don't like singing.

TRACK 49

1 Listen, read, and say.

2 Look and complete.

I ___don't like___ watching TV.

I ______________ playing board games.

I ______________ reading books.

I ______________ singing karaoke.

3 Number in order. Ask and answer.

you ◯ What (1) do ◯ doing? ◯ like ◯

I like playing board games.

WORKBOOK page 44

GRAMMAR GUIDE page 131

UNIT 6

Lesson 3

· SOUNDS GREAT ·

TRACK 50

1 Listen and chant.

It's rainy today.
Let's play a game.
Sit down with me.
Let's make a train!

TRACK 51

2 Listen, say, and color.

ai **ay**

rainy

play

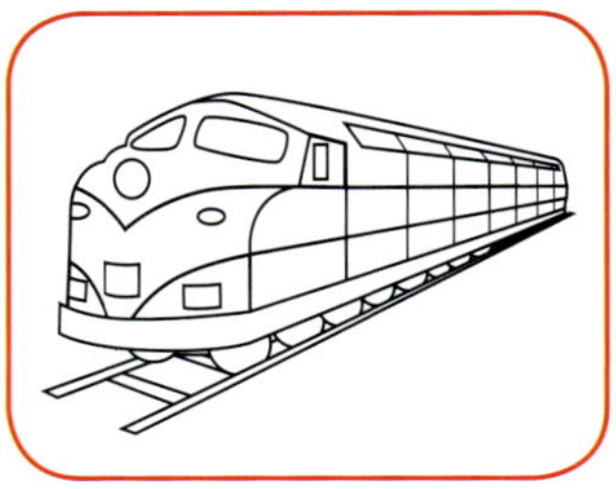

train

today

3 Look and write.

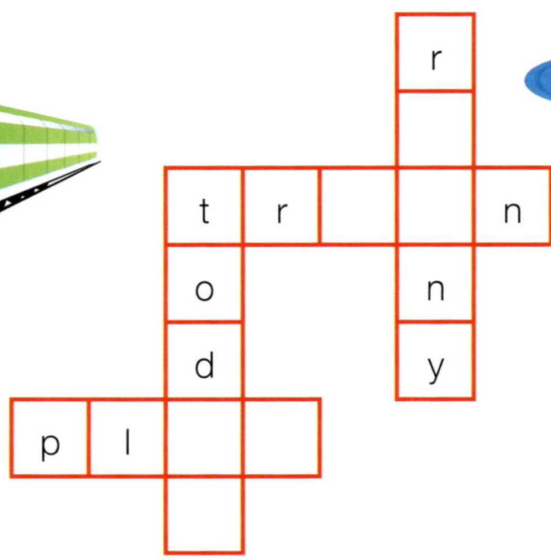

4 Read the chant and underline *ai* and *ay*.

WORKBOOK page 45

READING TIME

TRACK 52

1 Listen and read.

2 Read the story again. Check (✓) the value.

Value your friends. ◯ Play outdoors. ◯

3 What do you like doing with your friends?

reading ◯ playing soccer ◯ playing games ◯ watching TV ◯

WORKBOOK page 46

· VOCABULARY ·

TRACK 53

1 Listen, point, and say.

TRACK 54

2 Listen and write their names.

TEMPLATE 6

3 Complete, write, and say.

WORKBOOK page 47

Lesson 6

GRAMMAR

He / She likes read**ing**.
He / She doesn't like sing**ing**.

TRACK 55

1 Listen, read, and say.

2 Look and circle.

1 Bubba doesn't like singing. True / False

2 Niki likes listening to music. True / False

TRACK 56

3 Sing and act. **Playing with Friends**

He likes reading books at school.
She likes swimming in the pool.

But they both like playing with friends.
They both like playing with friends.

She doesn't like climbing a tree.
He doesn't like watching TV.

Chorus

WORKBOOK page 48

GRAMMAR GUIDE page 131

LET'S VISIT ARGENTINA

1 Read about a family from Argentina.

Hello! I'm Laura.
I'm nine years old, and I'm from Buenos Aires, in Argentina.

I like playing soccer. Soccer is very popular in Argentina. We love playing soccer and watching it on TV.

This is my grandmother and grandfather. My grandma's name is Flora, and my grandpa's name is Miguel. My grandma doesn't like playing soccer! But she likes listening to music, and she likes dancing the tango. It's her favorite dance.

Think Twice

1 Circle.

Flora likes **playing soccer** / **listening to music** / **dancing**.

2 Do you like dancing?

SPEAKING TIME

1 Draw, write, and say.

People in Argentina like dancing.
People in my country like
________________________.

NEW FRIENDS

1 Complete the conversation. Choose your response.

Hi. I like playing soccer.

I like playing soccer, too. ◯

I don't like playing soccer. I like ◯
________________________.

2 Act out the conversation.

WORKBOOK page 49

UNIT 5

PROGRESS CHECK

1 Look and write. Ask and answer.

Can he ______________________?

______________________.

Can he ______________________?

______________________.

Can she ______________________?

______________________.

2 Write *can* or *can't*.

1 Dogs ______________ do taekwondo.

2 Ducks ______________ swim.

3 Donkeys ______________ play the guitar.

4 Snakes ______________ fly.

5 Grasshoppers ______________ hop.

6 Cats ______________ climb trees.

THINK AGAIN!

People eat ______________________ and ______________________ in South Korea.

My favorite lesson is on page ______________________.

A musical instrument popular in South Korea is ______________________.

WORKBOOK page 50
STICKERS
PASSPORT page 10

UNIT 6

PROGRESS CHECK

1 Look and write.

I like playing board games.

____

____

____

____

____

2 Match.

He likes

She likes

She likes

He likes

She likes

He likes

listening to music.

watching TV.

drawing.

making models.

painting.

reading books.

THINK AGAIN!

A dance from Argentina is ______________________________.

My favorite picture is on page ______________________________.

A popular activity in Argentina is ______________________________.

WORKBOOK page 51

STICKERS

PASSPORT page 12

SOUTH KOREA

Janggu, a traditional Korean drum.

The *janggu* drum in a performance by a South Korean group.

Folk dancers with a *sogo* drum.

STEAM

TEAM NAME

What is sound? How does it travel?

1 Get materials.

cardboard

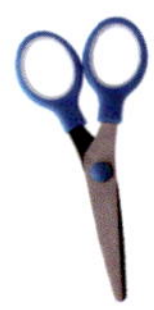

scissors

2 pieces of string

wooden stick

4 beads

markers

tape

2 Draw a cardboard circle. Cut it out.

A drum is a percussion instrument. It makes sound when hit. Drums can be very different in size and shape.

Korean CheonGo drum

djembe drum

spinning drum

CHALLENGE 3

MAKE A SPINNING DRUM

ARGENTINA

3 Ask an adult to make 2 small holes.

4 Add strings and beads.

5 Insert the stick into the cardboard circle and decorate.

6 Test your drum.

What kind of drum is traditional in your culture? How is it played?

Super Star Challenge

Play in a drum parade.

Bombo legüero, a traditional drum from Argentina.

The *bombo legüero* in an opening festival in Argentina.

A folk dance accompanied by *bombo legüero*.

TEAMWORK ★★★★★

UNIT 7

MONGOLIA

Which animal doesn't live in Mongolia? Check (✓).

1 

2 

3 

4 

UNIT 7

Lesson 1

· VOCABULARY ·

TRACK 57

1 Listen, point, and say.

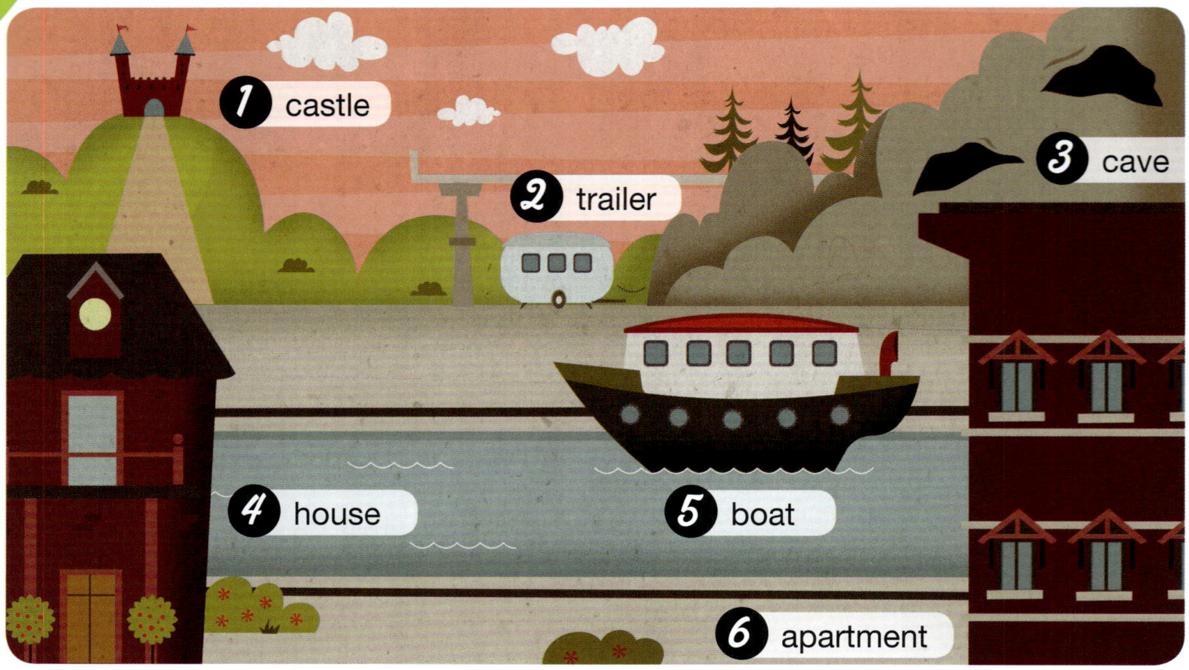

TRACK 58

2 Listen and say what's missing.

3 Draw your home and write.

This is ______________________________.

WORKBOOK page 52

Lesson 2

GRAMMAR

He / She / It lives in a house.

TRACK 59

1 Listen, read, and say.

2 Play the Card Game.

TEMPLATE 7

WORKBOOK page 53

GRAMMAR GUIDE page 132

· SOUNDS GREAT ·

TRACK 60

1 Listen and chant.

The birds fly high in the sky.
The birds love apple pie.

TRACK 61

2 Listen, say, and color.

igh **y** **ie**

pie | sky | fly | high

3 Write and match.

p ____ ____   h ____ ____ ____   sk ____   fl ____

4 Read the chant and underline *igh, y,* and *ie.*

WORKBOOK page 54

·READING TIME·

TRACK 62

1 Listen and read.

2 Read the story again. Check (✓) the **value**.

Welcome people. ◯ Talk to your neighbors. ◯

3 What do you say to a new boy or girl in your class? Circle.

Come and play with us. / Do you like spiders?

WORKBOOK page 55

UNIT 7

Lesson 5

VOCABULARY

TRACK 63

1 Listen, point, and say.

1 ocean

2 desert

3 jungle

4 woods

5 city

6 country

2 Find and circle.

<table>
<tr><td>n</td><td>w</td><td>e</td><td>l</td><td>t</td><td>q</td><td>i</td><td>f</td><td>c</td><td>s</td><td>a</td><td>o</td><td>l</td><td>n</td><td>w</td></tr>
<tr><td>c</td><td>o</td><td>u</td><td>n</td><td>t</td><td>r</td><td>y</td><td>g</td><td>i</td><td>n</td><td>e</td><td>c</td><td>v</td><td>p</td><td>i</td></tr>
<tr><td>a</td><td>o</td><td>z</td><td>c</td><td>y</td><td>m</td><td>c</td><td>s</td><td>t</td><td>g</td><td>k</td><td>e</td><td>i</td><td>j</td><td>o</td></tr>
<tr><td>f</td><td>d</td><td>e</td><td>s</td><td>e</td><td>r</td><td>t</td><td>b</td><td>y</td><td>c</td><td>f</td><td>a</td><td>u</td><td>m</td><td>p</td></tr>
<tr><td>m</td><td>s</td><td>p</td><td>d</td><td>m</td><td>s</td><td>e</td><td>l</td><td>h</td><td>j</td><td>u</td><td>n</td><td>g</td><td>l</td><td>e</td></tr>
</table>

3 Complete.

1 The iguana lives in the ____________________.

2 The bird lives in the ____________________.

3 The bear lives in the ____________________.

4 The fish lives in the ____________________.

5 The cow lives in the ____________________.

6 The monkey lives in the ____________________.

WORKBOOK page 56

GRAMMAR

Where do you live?
I live in the city.

TRACK 64

1 Listen, read, and say.

TRACK 65

2 Sing and act. **Where Do You Live?**

Where do you live?
I live in the desert.
The desert! The desert!
The sizzling fizzling desert!

Where do you live?
I live in the ocean.
The ocean! The ocean!
The splishy splashy ocean!

Where do you live?
I live in the city.
The city! The city!
The busy whizzy city!

WORKBOOK page 57

GRAMMAR GUIDE page 132

LET'S VISIT MONGOLIA

WELCOME TO MONGOLIA INTERNATIONAL AIRPORT TOURISM 23 • SEPT

1 Read about home life in Mongolia.

Hi! I'm Maa. Welcome to Mongolia! These are my parents.

We don't live in the city. We live in the country. And we don't live in an apartment. We live in a tent! This is our house. It's called a yurt. In Mongolia, a lot of families live in tents. Where do you live?

Think Twice

1 Circle.

In Mongolia, a lot of people live in yurts. True / False

2 Complete about your country.

houses boats trailers
castles apartments tents

In __________, a lot of people live in __________. Some people live in __________.

SPEAKING TIME

1 Draw, write, and say.

This is a tent in Mongolia.

This is a / an ____________ in my country.

NEW FRIENDS

1 Complete the conversation. Choose your response.

I live in the country. Where do you live?

I live in the ____________.

Come and play at my house.

OK. Thank you! ◯ I'd love to. ◯

2 Act out the conversation.

WORKBOOK page 58

UNIT 8

AUSTRALIA

TRACK 66

Listen and circle the traditional music from Australia.

1 2 3 4

UNIT 8

Lesson 1

VOCABULARY

TRACK 67

1 Listen, point, and say.

1 recorder

2 trumpet

3 drums

4 piano

5 violin

6 tambourine

TRACK 68

2 Listen and guess.

3 Act and say.

WORKBOOK page 59

GRAMMAR

Do you play board games?
Yes, **I do. /** No, **I don't.**

TRACK 69

1 Listen, read, and say.

2 Complete and circle.

1 Do you ______________________ the trumpet? Yes, I do. / No, I don't.

2 ______________________ play the drums? Yes, I do. / No, I don't.

3 Ask and answer.

the piano **the recorder** **the violin**
soccer **computer games** **board games**

Do you play the piano?

Yes, I do.

WORKBOOK page 60
GRAMMAR GUIDE page 132

Lesson 3

SOUNDS GREAT

TRACK 70

1 Listen and chant.

Put on your coat,
Get in the boat,
Sit down low,
And row, row, row!

TRACK 71

2 Listen, say, and color.

oa **ow**

boat

row

coat

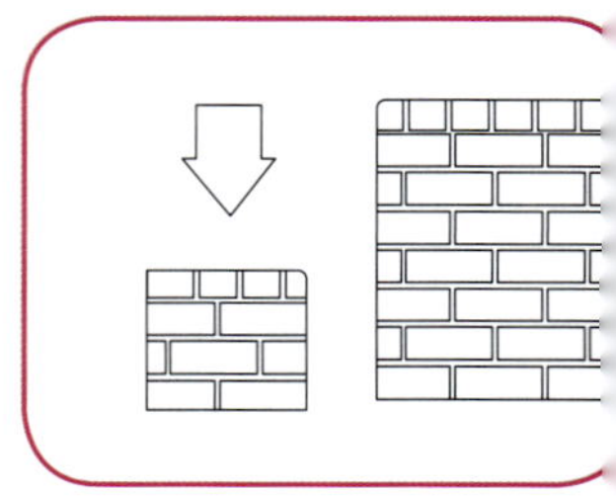

low

3 Look and write.

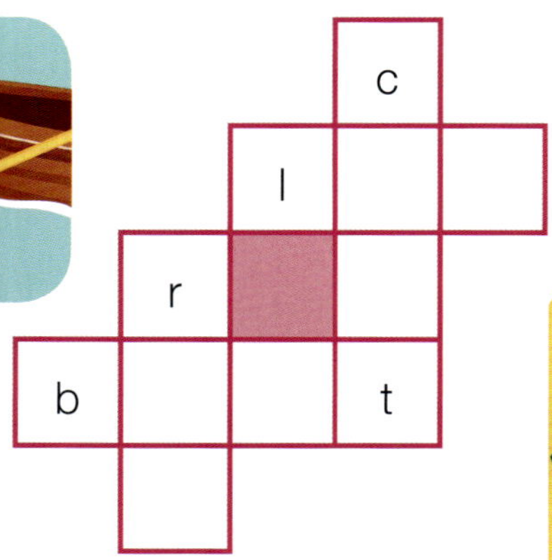

4 Read the chant and underline *oa* and *ow*.

WORKBOOK
page 61

READING TIME

TRACK 72

1 Listen and read.

2 Read the story again. Check (✓) the **value**.

Play an instrument. ◯ Help your friends. ◯

3 How do you help your friends? Circle.

I help my friends to **play computer games** / **make models** / **climb trees** / **do homework** / **spell**.

WORKBOOK page 62

Unit 8

Lesson 5

VOCABULARY

TRACK 73

1 Listen, point, and say.

TRACK 74

2 Listen and say what's next.

TEMPLATE 8

3 Make a chart and say.

WORKBOOK page 63

Lesson 6

TRACK 75

1 Listen, read, and say.

GRAMMAR

Does he / she play soccer **on** Tuesdays?

Yes, **he / she does.**

No, **he / she doesn't.**

TRACK 76

2 Sing and act. **Action Girl**

Does she play soccer on Mondays?
Does she play the trumpet on Tuesdays?
Yes, she does. Yes, she does.
She's an action girl.

Does she do taekwondo on Wednesdays?
Does she play the piano on Thursdays?
Yes, she does. Yes, she does.
She's an action girl.

Does she go to sleep on Fridays?
Does she go to sleep on Fridays?
Yes, she does. Yes, she does.
She's a very tired girl!

WORKBOOK page 64

GRAMMAR GUIDE page 132

LET'S VISIT AUSTRALIA

1 Read about a boy from Australia.

My name is Bahloo. I'm from Australia.

I like listening to and playing music. I'm a musician. I play the drums, the tambourine, and a special instrument called the didgeridoo. It's a traditional musical instrument from Australia.

After school, I play music on Mondays, Wednesdays, and Fridays. On Tuesdays and Thursdays, I draw pictures. On Saturdays and Sundays, I make models and I paint. I'm very creative!

Think Twice

1 What does Bahloo like doing? Circle.

painting / playing the drums / playing soccer / drawing / watching TV

2 Do you like music and art?

SPEAKING TIME

1 Draw, write, and say.

This is a musician from my country. He / She likes playing the ______________________.

NEW FRIENDS

1 Complete the conversation. Choose your response.

2 Act out the conversation.

WORKBOOK page 65

PROGRESS CHECK

1 Look, match, and write.

1 ______________________ in a cave.
2 ______________________ in a trailer.
3 ______________________ in a boat.
4 He lives in a castle.

2 Look and complete. Then ask and answer.

Where __________ you __________?

I ______________________ in the ______________________.

Where __________?

I ______________________ in ______________________.

THINK AGAIN!

A typical home in Mongolia is a ______________________.

My favorite lesson is on page ______________________.

An animal from Mongolia is ______________________.

WORKBOOK page 66
STICKERS
PASSPORT page 14

UNIT 8

PROGRESS CHECK

1 Write *Yes, I do.* or *No, I don't.*

1 Do you play the piano? ______________________.

2 Do you play the trumpet? ______________________.

3 Do you play the tambourine? ______________________.

4 Do you play the drums? ______________________.

5 Do you play the violin? ______________________.

6 Do you play the recorder? ______________________.

2 Look and write *Yes, he does.* or *No, he doesn't.*

1 Does he play the piano on Mondays? ______________________.

2 Does he play soccer on Thursdays? ______________________.

3 Does he play the trumpet on Fridays? ______________________.

4 Does he play with friends on Saturdays? ______________________.

5 Does he play the tambourine on Sundays? ______________________.

THINK AGAIN!

A traditional instrument from Australia is the ______________________.

My favorite picture is on page ______________________.

My favorite lesson is on page ______________________.

WORKBOOK page 67

STICKERS

PASSPORT page 16

MONGOLIA

This is a traditional home in Mongolia called a *ger*.

The wood is painted with patterns.

Neighbors live next to each other.

STEAM

TEAM NAME

Nomadic people move their home from place to place. Why do you think that is?

1. Get materials.

cardboard tube

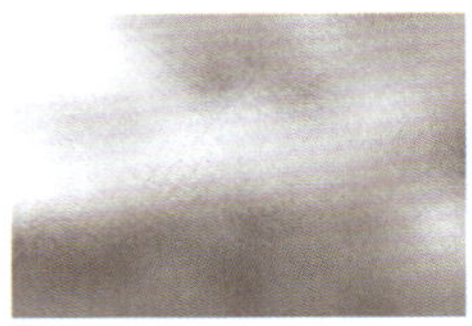

mirrored sheet

markers

tape

tracing paper

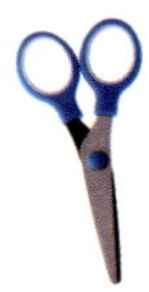

scissors

straw

2. Draw three rectangles on the mirrored sheet. Cut them out.

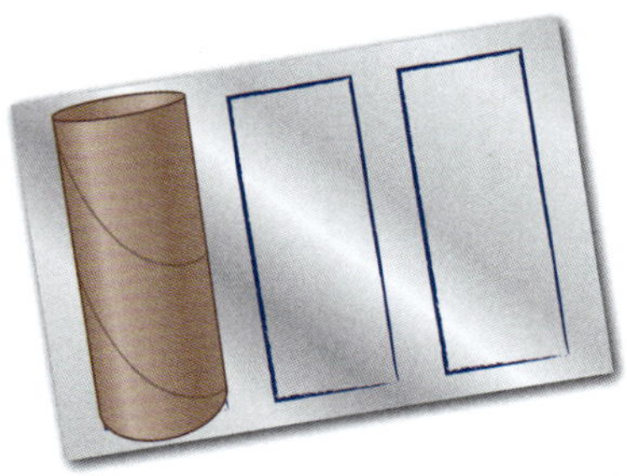

The patterns on the didgeridoo tell a story.

The patterns on the door are symbols of good wishes.

CHALLENGE 4

MAKE A KALEIDOSCOPE

AUSTRALIA

3 Tape and fold into a triangle.

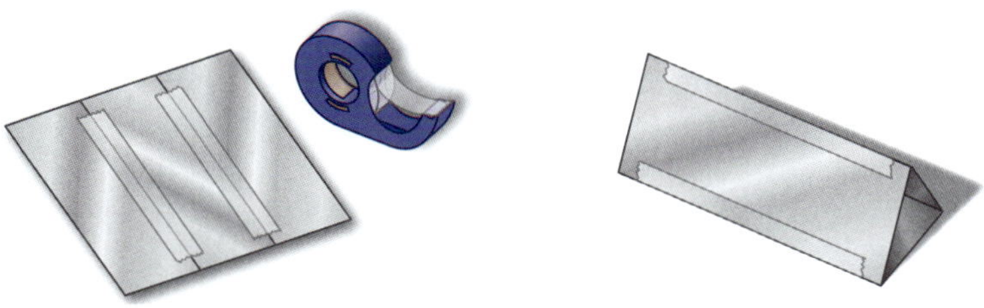

4 Put in tube.

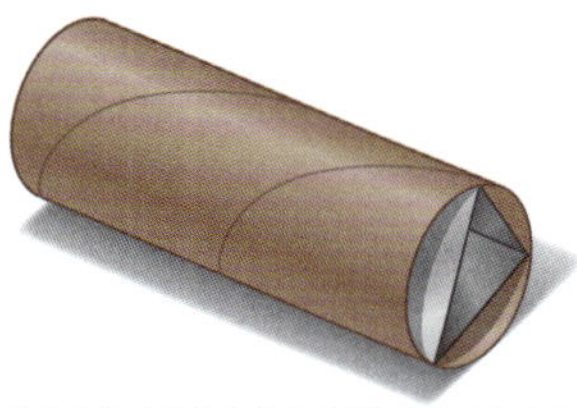

5 Cut straw and tape to top.

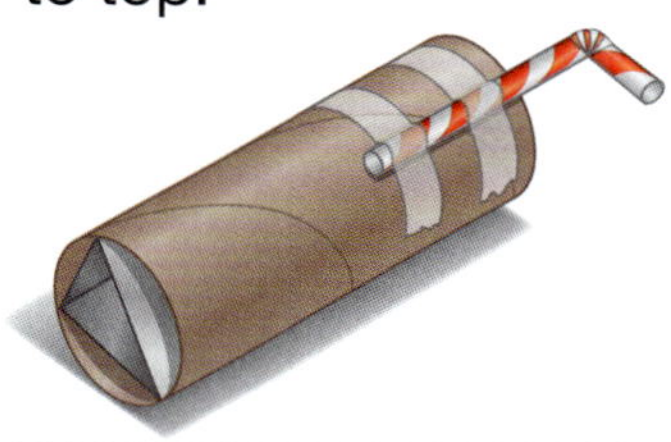

6 Decorate tracing paper with a pattern from Mongolia or Australia.

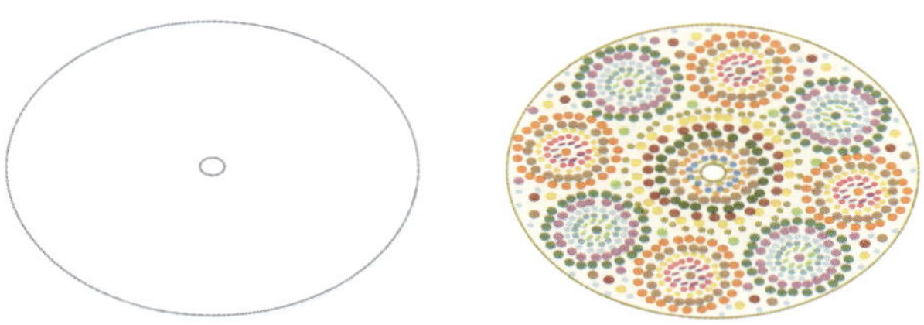

7 Attach pattern to straw. Look into the light!

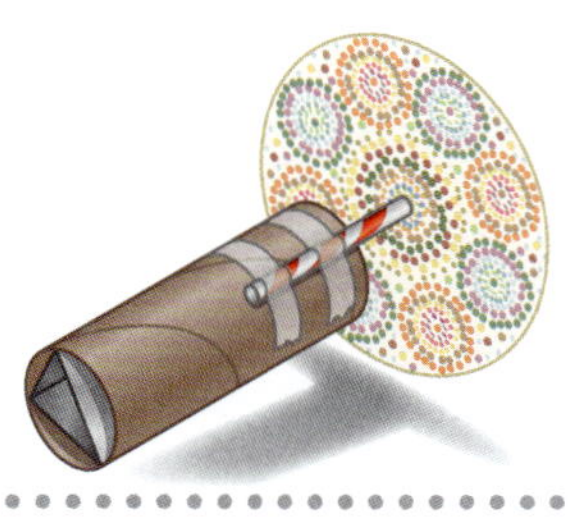

Which patterns are traditional in your country?

Super Star Challenge

Make a kaleidoscope pattern from a different culture.

Aboriginal people paint stories using small circles or dots.

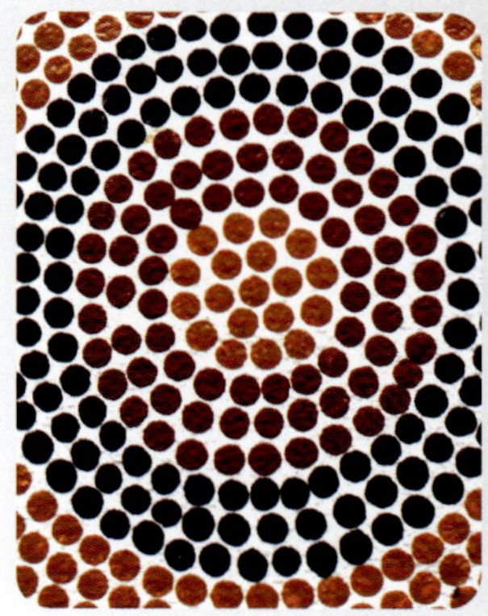

The dot designs fill the painting.

The colors come from nature.

THAILAND

UNIT 9

Check (✓) three other types of transportation used in Thailand.

UNIT 9

Lesson 1

VOCABULARY

TRACK 77

1 Listen, point, and say.

1 airplane

2 bus

3 helicopter

4 car

5 train

6 motorcycle

TRACK 78

2 Listen and guess.

3 Play the Memory Game.

WORKBOOK page 68

GRAMMAR

I don't go to school **by** train.
I go by bus.
He / She doesn't go to school **by** boat.
He / She goes by train.

TRACK 79

1 Listen, read, and say.

2 Complete.

1 He ________________ to school by bus.
He ________________ by train.

2 She ________________ to school by motorcycle.
She ________________ by bus.

3 Talk to a friend.

I don't go to school by bus. I go by car.

WORKBOOK page 69
GRAMMAR GUIDE page 133

SOUNDS GREAT

TRACK 80

1 Listen and chant.

Oh, no! My new blue shoe!
Here! I have some glue for you.

TRACK 81

2 Listen, say, and color.

ue **ew**

blue

glue

new

3 Write and match.

ue **ew**

bl ____ ____

gl ____ ____

n ____ ____

4 Read the chant and underline *ue* and *ew.*

WORKBOOK page 70

READING TIME

TRACK 82

1 Listen and read.

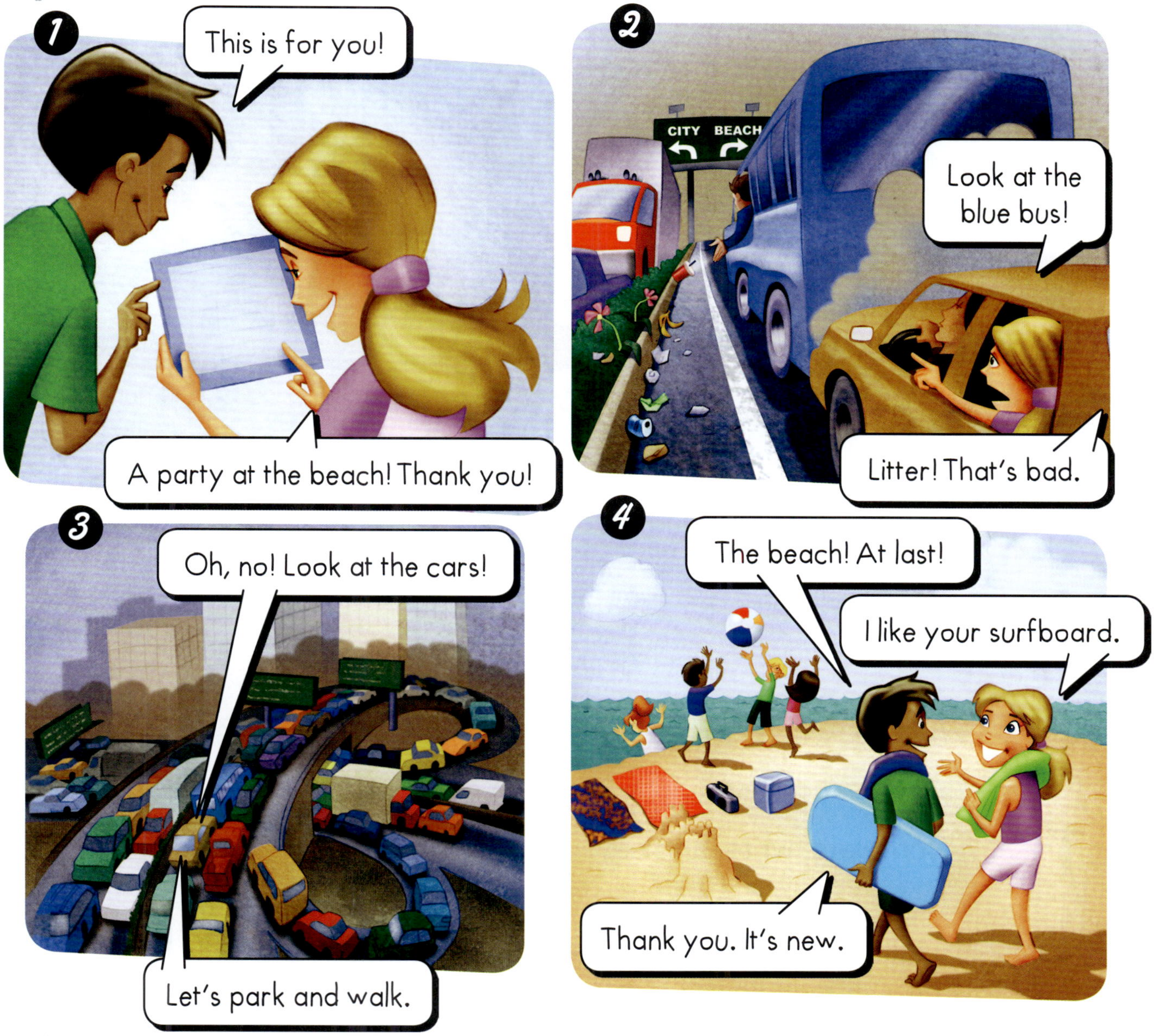

2 Read the story again. Check (✓) the value.

Care for the environment. ◯ Walk to the beach. ◯

3 How do you go to the local store? Circle.

WORKBOOK page 71

UNIT 9

Lesson 5

VOCABULARY

TRACK 83

1 Listen, point, and say.

10	20	30	40	50
ten	twenty	thirty	forty	fifty
60	70	80	90	100
sixty	seventy	eighty	ninety	one hundred

2 Match.

100   20   60   10   40   30

forty   twenty   one hundred   thirty   ten   sixty

TEMPLATE 9

3 Complete, write, and say.

WORKBOOK page 72

Lesson 6

GRAMMAR

How many apples **are there**?
There are twenty.

TRACK 84

1 Listen, read, and say.

2 Ask and answer.

pencils **chairs** **windows** **desks**

How many pencils are there?

There are nine.

TRACK 85

3 Sing. **The Picnic Box**

How many apples are there in the picnic box?
There are forty and two,
That makes forty-two …

How many sandwiches are there in the picnic box?
There are twenty and six,
That makes twenty-six …

How many cookies are there in the picnic box?
There are thirty and five,
That makes thirty-five …

WORKBOOK page 73
GRAMMAR GUIDE page 133

LET'S VISIT THAILAND

1 Read about city life in Thailand.

My name is Mali. I live in Bangkok. It's a city in Thailand.

There are a lot of cars, buses, trains, motorcycles, and taxis. Bangkok has special taxis.

Look at this one. It's called a tuk-tuk. It's very colorful. It's blue, yellow, and red. I go to school by tuk-tuk.

This is a taxi, too. It's a river taxi. Some people in Bangkok go to work by river taxi. And some people go to the market by river taxi, too. Are there river taxis in your city?

Think Twice

1 Circle.

Mali goes to school by **bus** / **taxi** / **tuk-tuk** / **river taxi.**

2 Are there different kinds of taxis in your country?

SPEAKING TIME

1 Draw, write, and say.

In Thailand, some people go to work by river taxi. In my country, some people go to work by ________________.

NEW FRIENDS

1 Complete the conversation. Choose your response.

Hello. I go to school by tuk-tuk. How do you go to school?

- I go to school by ________________ ◯
- I walk to school. ◯

2 Act out the conversation.

WORKBOOK page 74

UNIT 10

PERU

WELCOME TO
PERU
INTERNATIONAL AIRPORT
TOURISM
Welcome to Peru!
I like her clothes. Look at the colors.

Color the clothes to match the photo.

1

2

3

4

UNIT 10

Lesson 1

· VOCABULARY ·

TRACK 86

1 Listen, point, and say.

2 Read, color, and say.

They're blue pants.

It's a green sweater.

It's a pink skirt.

3 Find and circle.

o	b	v	g	m	y	u	z	l	p
s	n	e	a	k	e	r	s	i	a
h	f	m	k	t	c	j	h	p	n
o	q	b	i	x	s	k	i	r	t
e	l	p	y	a	c	m	r	o	s
s	w	b	s	w	e	a	t	e	r

WORKBOOK page 75

GRAMMAR

This is Maria's sweater.
These are Tom's books.

TRACK 87

1 Listen, read, and say.

2 Look and write.

1 These are ______________________ shoes.

2 This is ______________________ shirt.

3 Find some things and say.

WORKBOOK page 76

GRAMMAR GUIDE page 133

UNIT 10

Lesson 3

· SOUNDS GREAT ·

TRACK 88

1 Listen and chant.

New clothes for your birthday.
From your mother and me.
Let's sing "Happy Birthday."
One, two, three …

TRACK 89

2 Listen, say, and color.

th **th**

three

birthday

mother

clothes

3 Write ***th*** or ***th***.

mo ___ ___ er

___ ___ ree

clo ___ ___ es

bir ___ ___ day

4 Read the chant and underline *th.*

WORKBOOK page 77

READING TIME

TRACK 90

1 Listen and read.

2 Read the story again. Check (✓) the value.

Say "Thank you." ◯ Share with family and friends. ◯

3 What do you share with your family? Circle.

clothes / books / candy / bedroom / toys

WORKBOOK page 78

UNIT 10 Lesson 5

VOCABULARY

TRACK 91

1 Listen, point, and say.

2 Complete.

1 It's a ________________ skirt.

4 They're ________________ sneakers.

2 It's a ________________ shirt.

5 They're ________________ pants.

3 They're ________________ shoes.

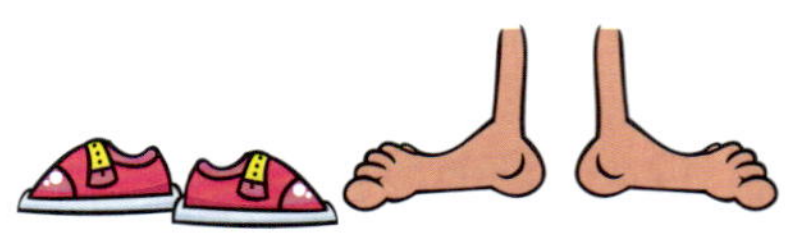

6 They're ________________ shoes.

3 Look and talk to a friend.

It's a long skirt.

They're short pants.

WORKBOOK page 79

GRAMMAR

He / She has an old guitar.

TRACK 92

1 Listen, read, and say.

2 Complete.

1 Bob ______________________ hat.

2 Alex ______________________ dog.

TRACK 93

TEMPLATE 10

3 Draw, color, and sing. **Our Clothes**

I have a new, new, new shirt.
She has an old, old, old skirt.
He has big, big, big sneakers.
I have small, small, small shoes.
We like our clothes!
We like our clothes!

WORKBOOK page 80

GRAMMAR GUIDE page 133

LET'S VISIT PERU

WELCOME TO PERU INTERNATIONAL AIRPORT TOURISM

1 Read about musical instruments from Peru.

I'm Pedro and I'm from Cusco, Peru.

Peru is famous for musical instruments. This is my musical instrument. It's called the pan pipes. The music is very beautiful. The pipes are short and long.

This is my sister. She plays a special guitar from Peru. It's very small, and it's old. My sister likes playing this guitar. She doesn't like playing big guitars. She can play the guitar and the pan pipes.

Think Twice

1 Circle.
Pedro can play the guitar and the pan pipes. True / False

2 Do you like music?

SPEAKING TIME

1 Draw, write, and say.

This is a special musical instrument from my country. It's called a ______________.

NEW FRIENDS

1 Complete the conversation. Choose your response.

Hello. I like playing the pan pipes. Do you like listening to traditional music?

Yes, I do. ◯

Not really. I prefer ______________. ◯

2 Act out the conversation.

WORKBOOK page 81

UNIT 9

PROGRESS CHECK

1 Complete.

1 He doesn't go to school by motorcycle.
He goes by bike.

2 ______ to school by bus.
______ by car.

3 ______ to school by helicopter.
______ by train.

4 ______ to school by airplane.
______ by taxi.

2 Write. Then ask and answer.

How many butterflies are there?

1 20  + 7  = 27 butterflies

There are twenty-seven.

2 50  + 2  = ______

3 70  + 1  = ______

4 40  + 7  = ______

THINK AGAIN!

A type of transportation in Thailand is ______.

My favorite lesson is on page ______.

A city in Thailand is ______.

WORKBOOK page 82
STICKERS
PASSPORT page 18

UNIT 10

PROGRESS CHECK

1 Complete and say.

1 Fiona has a long skirt.

2 Rosy has a ________________.

3 Fiona has an ________________.

4 Rosy has a ________________.

Fiona and Rosy.

2 Write.

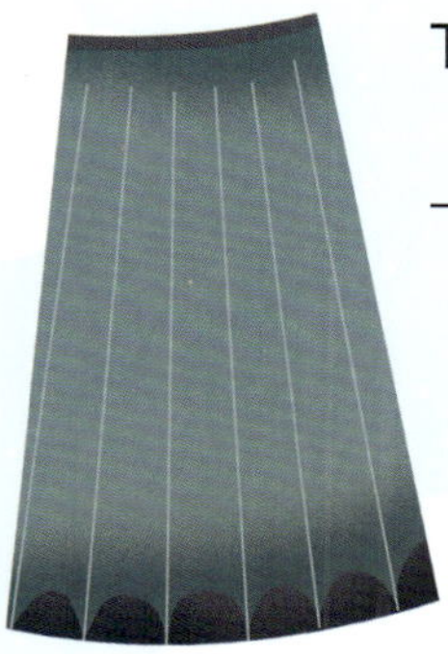

This is

Fiona's skirt.

This is

________________.

These are

________________.

This is

________________.

THINK AGAIN!

A musical instrument from Peru is ________________.

My favorite picture is on page ________________.

Clothes people wear in Peru are ________________.

WORKBOOK page 83

STICKERS

PASSPORT page 20

THAILAND

Paknam temple and Khlong-Dan river, Bangkok.

Amphawa floating market, Bangkok.

The boats in the floating market are small and made of wood.

STEAM

TEAM NAME

Make predictions about objects that will float or sink.

float	sink

1 Select the materials you need to design your boat.

Many Thai boats are decorated with colored ribbons and flowers to pay respect to water spirits.

Some Uru boats have a feline figurehead on the bow. The puma is a sacred animal for the Andean peoples.

CHALLENGE 5

· FLOAT YOUR BOAT ·

❷ Design and build a boat. Look at some examples.

❸ Test your boat. Does it sink or float?

____

❹ Add coins to your boat. Does it sink or float?

____

❺ Draw your boat.

What makes the water a good or a bad place to live?

Super Star Challenge

Work together to design a floating island.

PERU

The Uru people live on the islands of Lake Titicaca.

The islands are made of reeds.

Balsas are boats made of dried reeds.

GRAMMAR GUIDE

HOW TO USE THE GRAMMAR GUIDE

GRANT'S HOME STUDY GUIDE

1 Read your grammar guide again at home.
2 Look at the example. Close your book. Try to say the example.
3 Open your book and check.

1 After your grammar lessons, turn to the Grammar Guide. Look at the example.

Sit down, please.
Don't talk.

2 Complete the activity.

Complete.

1 Stand ___up___, please.
2 Don't sit ________.
3 Clean up, ________________.
4 ________ shout.

3 Check your answers.

UNIT 1 CANADA

Lesson 2

Sit down, please.
Don't run.

Complete.

1 Stand ____________, please.

2 Don't sit ____________.

3 Clean up, ____________.

4 ____________ shout.

Lesson 6

How do you
spell your name?

Complete.

1 How ________ you spell "snake"?

2 ________ do you ________ "panda"?

3 ________ ________ you spell "clock"?

4 ________ do you ________ your name? ____________

UNIT 2 GERMANY

Lesson 2

What time is it?
It's eight **o'clock.**

Complete.

1 What ________ is it? It's three ____________.

2 ________ ________ is it? ________ two o'clock.

3 What time ________ ________?
________ five ____________.

Lesson 6

I get up **at**
six **o'clock.**

Complete.

1 I get ________ at ________ o'clock.

2 I have lunch at ________ ____________.

3 I ________ dinner at ________ ____________ in the evening.

4 I go to bed ________ ________ o'clock at night.

3 KENYA

Lesson 2

This is a goat.
That's a donkey.
These are chickens.
Those are cows.

Complete.

1 That's ________ chicken.

2 This ________ ________ sheep.

3 Those ________ birds.

4 These ________ ducks.

Lesson 6

What's this / that? — **It's a** ladybug / **an** ant.

What are these / those? — **They're** caterpillars.

Complete.

1 ________ that?

2 ________ ________ ant.

3 What ________ those?

4 ________ grasshoppers.

4 TURKEY

Lesson 2

Do you like tomatoes?
Yes, **I do**. / No, **I don't**.

Complete.

1 ________ you like onions? Yes, I ________.

2 Do you ________ beans? ________, I do.

3 Do ________ like ants? No, I ________.

4 Do you like ________? ________, I don't.

Lesson 6

I like pancakes.
I don't like peppers.

Complete.

1 I ________ carrots.

2 I ________ pancakes.

3 I ________ peppers.

4 I ________ cookies.

UNIT 5 SOUTH KOREA

Lesson 2

Can you speak Vietnamese?

Yes, I can. /
No, I can't.

Complete.

1 ________ you play the guitar?

________, I can.

2 Can ________ jump rope? No, I

________.

3 Can you touch your toes?

________________.

4 Can you climb a tree?

________________.

Lesson 6

I / He / She / They can sing.
I / He / She / They can't swim.

Complete.

1 Dogs ________________ sing.

2 Birds ________________ sing.

3 Dogs ________________ fly.

4 Birds ________________ fly.

UNIT 6 ARGENTINA

Lesson 2

What do you like doing?
I like play**ing** soccer.
I don't like
watch**ing** TV.

Complete.

1 What ________ you like ________?

2 I ________ reading.

3 I ________ like playing soccer.

4 I ________________________.

Lesson 6

He / She likes paint**ing**.
He / She doesn't like swimm**ing**.

Complete. Write about your friend.

1 He / She likes ________________.

2 He / She doesn't like ________________.

3 He / She ________________________.

UNIT 7 MONGOLIA

Lesson 2

He / She / It lives in a house boat.

Write the words in order.

1 She castle lives a in

_______________________________.

2 trailer a in He lives

_______________________________.

3 in lives cave It a

_______________________________.

Lesson 6

Where do you live?
I live in the country.

Complete.

1 ________ do you live?

2 I ________ in the city.

3 Where ________ you ________?

4 I live ________ ________ jungle.

UNIT 8 AUSTRALIA

Lesson 2

Do you play the guitar?
Yes, **I do**. /
No, **I don't**.

Complete.

1 ________ you play the violin? Yes, I ________.

2 Do ________ play the piano? ________, I don't.

3 ________ you ________ soccer? ________, ________ do.

Lesson 6

Does he / she play soccer **on** Tuesdays?
Yes, **he / she does**.
No, **he / she doesn't**.

Complete.

1 ________ he go to the park on Tuesdays? ________, he doesn't.

2 Does ________ play soccer ________ Mondays? Yes, he ________.

3 ________ he ________ to the mall ________ Thursdays? No, ________ ________.

9 THAILAND

Lesson 2

I don't go to school **by** train.
I go by bus.
He / She doesn't go to school **by** bus.
He / She goes by bike.

Complete.

1 ________ doesn't go to school by train. He ________ by bus.

2 She ________ go to school ________ bike. ________ goes ________ bus.

3 I don't ______________________.
I ______________________.

Lesson 6

How many pencils **are there**?
There are twenty-four.

Complete.

1 How many apples are ________? ________ are eight.

2 ________ many bananas ________ there? There ________ four.

3 ________ ________ cookies are there? ________ ________ ten.

10 PERU

Lesson 2

This is Maria's backpack.
These are Maria's books.

Complete.

1 This ________ Maria's skirt.

2 ________ are Tom's books.

3 ________ is Alan's shirt.

4 These ________ Grant's sneakers.

Lesson 6

He / She has an old guitar.

Write the words in order.

1 He big has hat a

______________________.

2 has short He pants

______________________.

3 new has sneakers He

______________________.

Adapted by Viv Lambert
Grammar Guide written by Viv Lambert
STEAM Challenge sections written by Sarah Elizabeth Sprague
Next Move is a registered trademark, property of Macmillan Publishers, 2013
First edition entitled "Next Stop" published 2009 by Macmillan Publishers

Director of Languages Brazil: Patrícia Souza De Luccia
Publishing Manager and Field Researcher: Patricia Muradas
Content Creation Coordinator: Cristina do Vale
Art Editor: Jean Aranha
Lead Editors: Ana Beatriz da Costa Moreira, Daniela Gonçala da Costa, Luciana Pereira da Silva
Content Editors: Millyane M. Moura Moreira, Tarsílio Soares Moreira
Digital Editor: Ana Paula Girardi
Editorial Assistant: Roberta Somera
Editorial Intern: Bruna Marques
Art Assistant: Denis Araujo
Art Intern: Jacqueline Alves
Graphic Production: Tatiane Romano, Thais Mendes P. Galvão
Proofreaders: Edward Willson, Márcia Leme, Sabrina Cairo Bileski
Design Concept: Design Divertido Artes Gráficas
Page Make-Up: Figurattiva Editorial
Photo Research: Marcia Sato
Image Processing: Jean Aranha, Jacqueline Alves, Denis Araujo
Audio: Argila Music, Núcleo de Criação
Cover Concept: Jean Aranha
Cover photography: TommL/iStockphoto/Getty Images, Bubert/iStockphoto/Getty Images, LokFung/iStockphoto/Getty Images.
Commissioned photography: Macmillan Publishers Ltd/Paul Bricknell (p. 10, 11, 14, 21, 25, 35, 48, 58, 62, 72, 83, 92, 96, 106, 110, 117, 121).
Map: Allmaps
Illustrations: Adilson Secco (p. 31, 55, 78-79, 102-103), Andrew Painter (p. 7, 11, 15, 17, 18, 21, 25, 35, 39, 45, 49, 53, 59, 63, 69, 73, 83, 87, 93, 97, 100, 107, 111, 117, 121), Anna Godwin (p. 12, 22, 36, 46, 60, 70, 84, 94, 108), Anthony Rule (p.128), David Hurtado (p. 23, 109, 129, 130, 131, 132, 133), Fiona Gowen (p. 37, 118), Harrington Illustration (p. 13, 23, 37, 47, 61, 71, 85, 95, 109, 119), Jim Peacock (p. 15, 20, 21, 28, 29, 53, 58, 63, 72, 73, 76, 77, 96, 100, 101, 110, 120, 124), Rita Giannetti | Sylvie Poggio (p. 20, 34, 35, 48, 49, 52, 53, 82, 97, 111, 124, 125).

We would like to dedicate this book to teachers all over Brazil. We would also like to thank our clients and teachers who have helped us make this book better with their many rich contributions and feedback straight from the classroom!

The authors and publishers would like to thank the following for permission to reproduce the photographic material:
p. 8: CanadaFirst/iStockphoto/Getty Images; p. 10: jaroon/iStockphoto/Getty Images, sam74100/iStockphoto/Getty Images, skynesher/iStockphoto/Getty Images, lissart/iStockphoto/Getty Images, szefei/iStockphoto/Getty Images, Julialine/iStockphoto/Getty Images; p. 16: FamVeld/iStockphoto/Getty Images, Mirceax/iStockphoto/Getty Images; p. 19: Tim Graham/Getty Images; p. 24: LittleBee80/iStockphoto/Getty Images, Wavebreakmedia/iStockphoto/Getty Images, djedzura/iStockphoto/Getty Images, SolStock/iStockphoto/Getty Images, Monkeybusinessimages/iStockphoto/Getty Images, LittleBee80/iStockphoto/Getty Images, Voyagerix/iStockphoto/Getty Images; p. 26: ferrantraite/iStockphoto/Getty Images, LauriPatterson/iStockphoto/Getty Images; p. 30: alexsl/iStockphoto/Getty Images, AK2/iStockphoto/Getty Images, Michel Loiselle, bgrier/iStockphoto/Getty Images, KeithBinns/iStockphoto/Getty Images, Professor25/iStockphoto/Getty Images, Nanniie_iiuu/iStockphoto/Getty Images, Andrey_Kuzmin/iStockphoto/Getty Images, Punkbarby/iStockphoto/Getty Images, Eduard Lysenko/iStockphoto/Getty Images, Michael Burrell/iStockphoto/Getty Images, Tolga TEZCAN/iStockphoto/Getty Images, Ralf Menache/iStockphoto/Getty Images; p. 31: 221A/iStockphoto/Getty Images, nedomacki/iStockphoto/Getty Images, Claudio Caridi/iStockphoto/Getty Images, KenWiedemann/iStockphoto/Getty Images; p. 32: elmvilla/iStockphoto/Getty Images; p. 33: AWM_Bonke/iStockphoto/Getty Images, wakila/iStockphoto/Getty Images, Image Source/iStockphoto/Getty Images, fieldwork/iStockphoto/Getty Images; p. 38: AlexStar/iStockphoto/Getty Images, ithinksky/iStockphoto/Getty Images, arlindo71/iStockphoto/Getty Images, doug4537/iStockphoto/Getty Images, Liliboas/iStockphoto/Getty Images, Anest/iStockphoto/Getty Images, luckyraccoon/iStockphoto/Getty Images; p. 40: vlad_karavaev/iStockphoto/Getty Images, Rob Pauley/iStockphoto/Getty Images, Jonathan Ross/iStockphoto/Getty Images, brytta/iStockphoto/Getty Images; p. 43: sfe-co2/iStockphoto/Getty Images, flapbocco/iStockphoto/Getty Images, gofotograf/iStockphoto/Getty Images, sasaperic/iStockphoto/Getty Images, Levent Konuk/iStockphoto/Getty Images; p. 44: Olga Danylenko/iStockphoto/Getty Images, yay micro/Easypix, Razvan/iStockphoto/Getty Images, digitalr/iStockphoto/Getty Images, kolesnikovserg/iStockphoto/Getty Images, Ekaterina_Lin/iStockphoto/Getty Images; p. 50: narvikk/iStockphoto/Getty Images, talip/iStockphoto/Getty Images, tataks/iStockphoto/Getty Images; p. 54: liangpv/iStockphoto/Getty Images, WLDavies/iStockphoto/Getty Images, Bartosz Hadyniak/iStockphoto/Getty Images, urosr/iStockphoto/Getty Images, Pazhyna/iStockphoto/Getty Images,Photokanok/iStockphoto/Getty Images, GlobalP/iStockphoto/Getty Images, PhotoEuphoria/iStockphoto/Getty Images, design56/iStockphoto/Getty Images, Max2611/iStockphoto/Getty Images, JackF/iStockphoto/Getty Images; p. 55: liangpv/iStockphoto/

Getty Images, graphixel/iStockphoto/Getty Images, florin1961/iStockphoto/Getty Images, Anadolu Agency/ Getty Images; p. 56: pius99/iStockphoto/Getty Images; p. 62: marcutti/iStockphoto/Getty Images, hanapon1002/ iStockphoto/Getty Images, LumineImages/iStockphoto/ Getty Images, PeopleImages/iStockphoto/Getty Images, SerrNovik/iStockphoto/Getty Images, Trout55/iStockphoto/ Getty Images; p. 64: Sirikornt/iStockphoto/Getty Images, ma-no/iStockphoto/Getty Images, Alamy/Fotoarena; p. 65: Carl Court/Getty Images; p. 66: holgs/iStockphoto/Getty Images; p. 67: Alamy/Fotoarena, Gerville/iStockphoto/ Getty Images, ozgurdonmaz/iStockphoto/Getty Images, Alamy/Fotoarena; p. 68: szirtesi/iStockphoto/Getty Images, AndreyPopov/iStockphoto/Getty Images, Neustockimages/iStockphoto/Getty Images, iofoto/ iStockphoto/Getty Images, Wavebreakmedia/iStockphoto/ Getty Images, nd3000/iStockphoto/Getty Images, Tolikoff Photography/iStockphoto/Getty Images, DragonImages/ iStockphoto/Getty Images, arekmalang/iStockphoto/Getty Images; p. 74: Choreograph/iStockphoto/Getty Images, yacobchuk/iStockphoto/Getty Images; p. 78: liangpv/ iStockphoto/Getty Images, Im Yeongsik/iStockphoto/ Getty Images, valentinrussanov/iStockphoto/Getty Images, vanbeets/iStockphoto/Getty Images, TwilightShow/ iStockphoto/Getty Images, Ziva_K/iStockphoto/Getty Images, deepblue4you/iStockphoto/Getty Images, Eduard Lysenko/iStockphoto/Getty Images, Marco Tulio/iStockphoto/Getty Images, RusN/iStockphoto/ Getty Images, Phawintphat/iStockphoto/Getty Images, chromatos/iStockphoto/Getty Images, tttuna/iStockphoto/ Getty Images, malerapaso/iStockphoto/Getty Images, svrid79/iStockphoto/Getty Images, pius99/iStockphoto/ Getty Images; p. 79: diverroy/iStockphoto/Getty Images, piccaya/iStockphoto/Getty Images, piccaya/iStockphoto/ Getty Images, Alamy/Fotoarena; p. 80: Lucy Brown/ iStockphoto/Getty Images, Goddard_Photography/ iStockphoto/Getty Images, namibelephant/iStockphoto/ Getty Images, Windofchange64/iStockphoto/Getty Images, afhunta/iStockphoto/Getty Images; p. 86: DarrenMower/iStockphoto/Getty Images, VSFP/ iStockphoto/Getty Images, hectojcm/iStockphoto/Getty Images, LuCaAr/iStockphoto/Getty Images, scaliger/ iStockphoto/Getty Images, RuudMorijn/iStockphoto/Getty Images; p. 88: Rawpixel/iStockphoto/Getty Images, Tuul & Bruno Morandi/Getty Images, withgod/iStockphoto/ Getty Images; p. 89: molloykeith/iStockphoto/Getty Images; p. 90: Ida Jarosova/iStockphoto/Getty Images; p. 92: Bronwyn8/iStockphoto/Getty Images, istudio5/ iStockphoto/Getty Images, ajkkafe/iStockphoto/Getty Images, Wavebreakmedia/iStockphoto/Getty Images, Wavebreakmedia/iStockphoto/Getty Images, Martinan/ iStockphoto/Getty Images; p. 98: Lonely Planet Images/ Getty Images, Violetastock/iStockphoto/Getty Images, Paul Patton/iStockphoto/Getty Images; p. 102: Panya-/ iStockphoto/Getty Images, Bartosz Hadyniak/iStockphoto/ Getty Images, bizoo_n/iStockphoto/Getty Images, gionnixxx/iStockphoto/Getty Images, zelg/iStockphoto/ Getty Images,UIG/Glow Images, Beto Celli, Lemon_tm/ iStockphoto/Getty Images, letoosen/iStockphoto/Getty Images, chromatos/iStockphoto/Getty Images, Coprid/ iStockphoto/Getty Images, Michael Burrell/iStockphoto/ Getty Images, Eduard Lysenko/iStockphoto/Getty Images, koya79/iStockphoto/Getty Images; p. 103: bodrumsurf/ iStockphoto/Getty Images, Photoresearchers/Latinstock, kira_an/iStockphoto/Getty Images, Lonely Planet Images/ iStockphoto/Getty Images, kira_an/iStockphoto/Getty Images; p. 104: nimon_t/iStockphoto/Getty Images; p. 105: tbradford/iStockphoto/Getty Images, Halfpoint/ iStockphoto/Getty Images, ayaka_photo/iStockphoto/ Getty Images, olaser/iStockphoto/Getty Images; p. 106: Travellinglight/iStockphoto/Getty Images, mladn61/ iStockphoto/Getty Images, Balefire9/iStockphoto/Getty Images, Tramino/iStockphoto/Getty Images, sculpies/ iStockphoto/Getty Images, Ljupco/iStockphoto/Getty Images; p. 112: pat138241/iStockphoto/Getty Images, intek1/iStockphoto/Getty Images, Leonardo Monteverde/ iStockphoto/Getty Images; p. 114: Bartosz Hadyniak/ iStockphoto/Getty Images; p. 116: GaryAlvis/iStockphoto/ Getty Images, kunchit2512/iStockphoto/Getty Images, popovaphoto/iStockphoto/Getty Images, NYS444/ iStockphoto/Getty Images, popovaphoto/iStockphoto/ Getty Images, PaulPaladin/iStockphoto/Getty Images; p. 122: hadynyah/iStockphoto/Getty Images, cuklom/ iStockphoto/Getty Images, Jose Girarte/iStockphoto/ Getty Images; p. 126: liangpv/iStockphoto/Getty Images, NicolasMcComber/iStockphoto/Getty Images, Photoprofi30/iStockphoto/Getty Images, enviromantic/ iStockphoto/Getty Images,letty17/iStockphoto/Getty Images,viviamo/iStockphoto/Getty Images, izusek/ iStockphoto/Getty Images,RTimages/iStockphoto/ Getty Images, vuk8691/iStockphoto/Getty Images, Uwe-Bergwitz/iStockphoto/Getty Images, photka/iStockphoto/ Getty Images, imon_t/iStockphoto/Getty Images; p. 127: VanReeel/iStockphoto/Getty Images, hadynyah/ iStockphoto/Getty Images, 1001nights/iStockphoto/Getty Images, traveler1116/iStockphoto/Getty Images.

Dados Internacionais de Catalogação na Publicação (CIP)

Bibliotecária responsável: Aline Graziele Benitez CRB-1/3129

C23n Cant, Amanda

1.ed. Next Station 2: Student's Book / Amanda Cant, Mary Charrington, Sarah Elizabeth Sprague; [Adapt.] Viv Lambert. – 1.ed. – São Paulo: Macmillan Education do Brasil, 2020.

136 p.; il.; 21 x 27 cm. – (Coleção Next Station)

ISBN: 978-85-511-0128-5

1. Língua inglesa. I. Charrington, Mary. II. Sprague, Sarah Elizabeth. III. Lambert, Viv. IV. Título. V. Série.

CDD 420

Índice para catálogo sistemático:

1. Língua inglesa

MACMILLAN EDUCATION DO BRASIL
Av. Brigadeiro Faria Lima, 1.309, 3º Andar –
Jd. Paulistano – São Paulo – SP – 01452-002
www.macmillan.com.br
Customer Service: [55] (11) 4613-2278
0800 16 88 77
Fax: [55] (11) 4612-6098

Impresso no Brasil, Maistype - 02/2025.

MISTO
Papel
FSC FSC® C041155

·MAP STICKERS·

PASSPORT STICKERS